WRITE YOU NAME WITH.

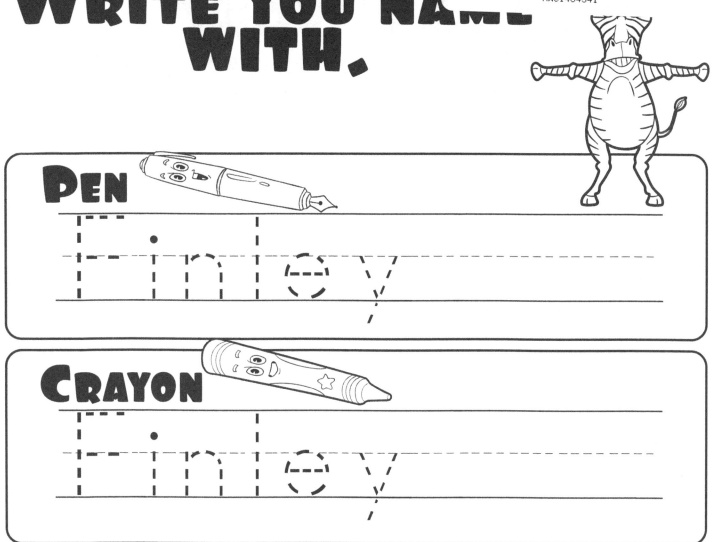

PEN

Finley

CRAYON

Finley

WRITE YOUR NAME IN BLUE

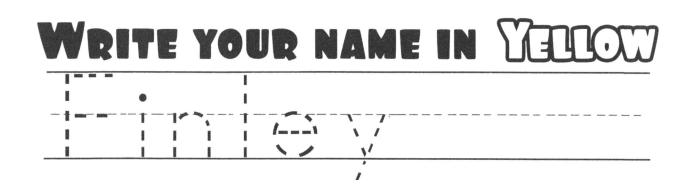

Finley

WRITE YOUR NAME IN YELLOW

Finley

DRAW YOUR FAVORITE THINGS

COLOR

FOOD

TOY

ANIMAL

MY NAME

My name starts with	My name ends with
_____	_____

FILL THE LETTERS OF YOUR NAME WHITH DIFFERENT COLORS

P B W F V I T
D E S Z N L C
J R A Y Q K
G U X O H M

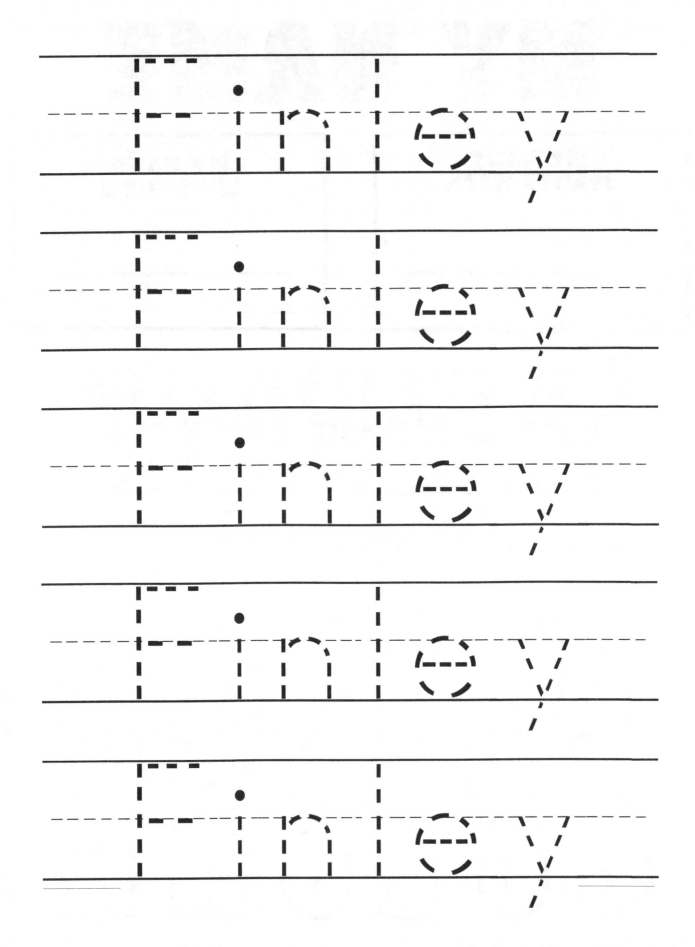

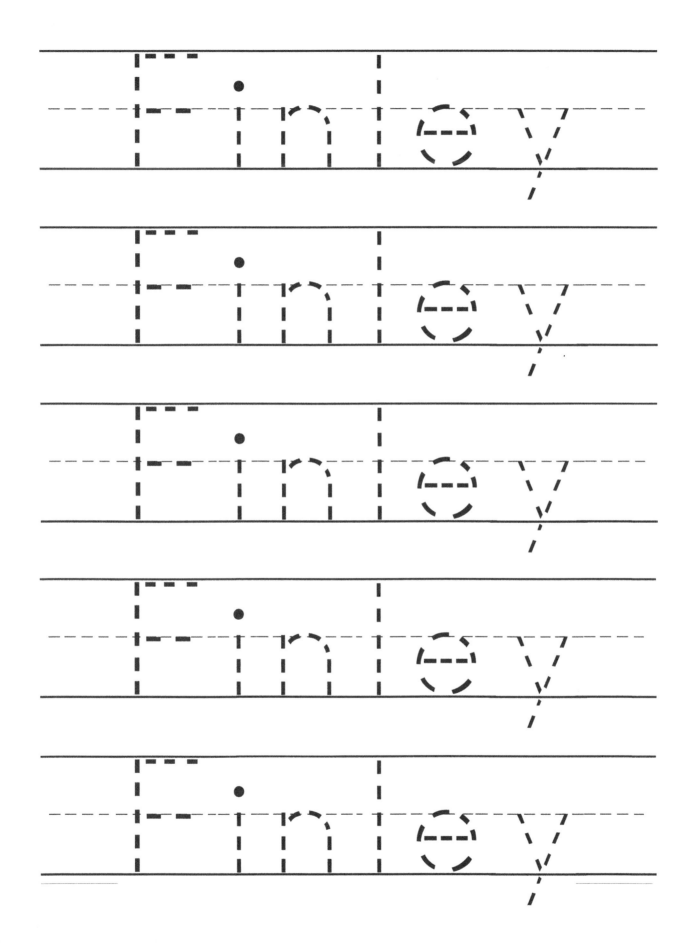

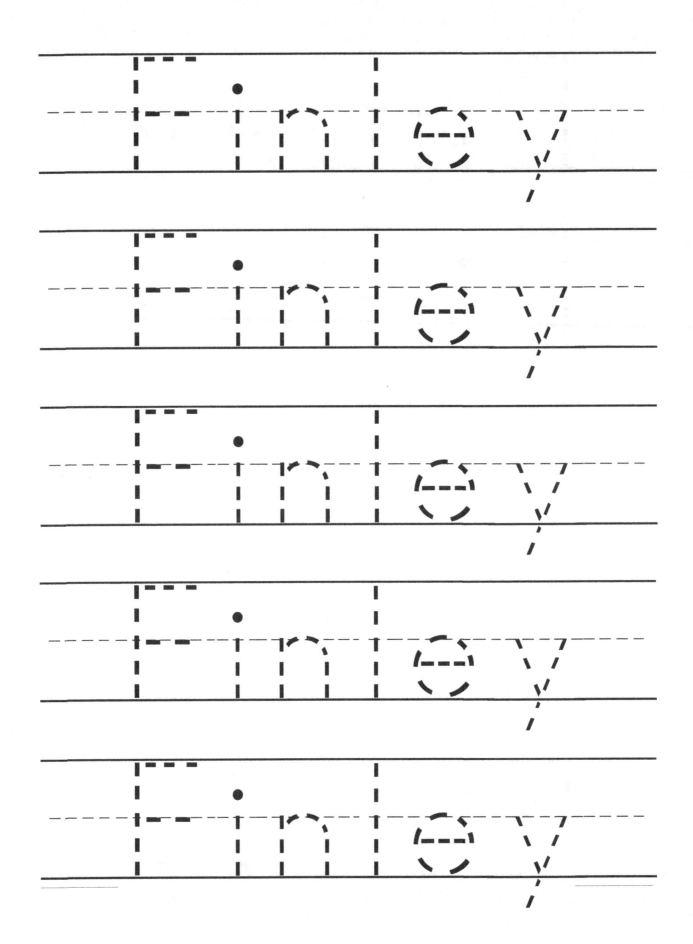

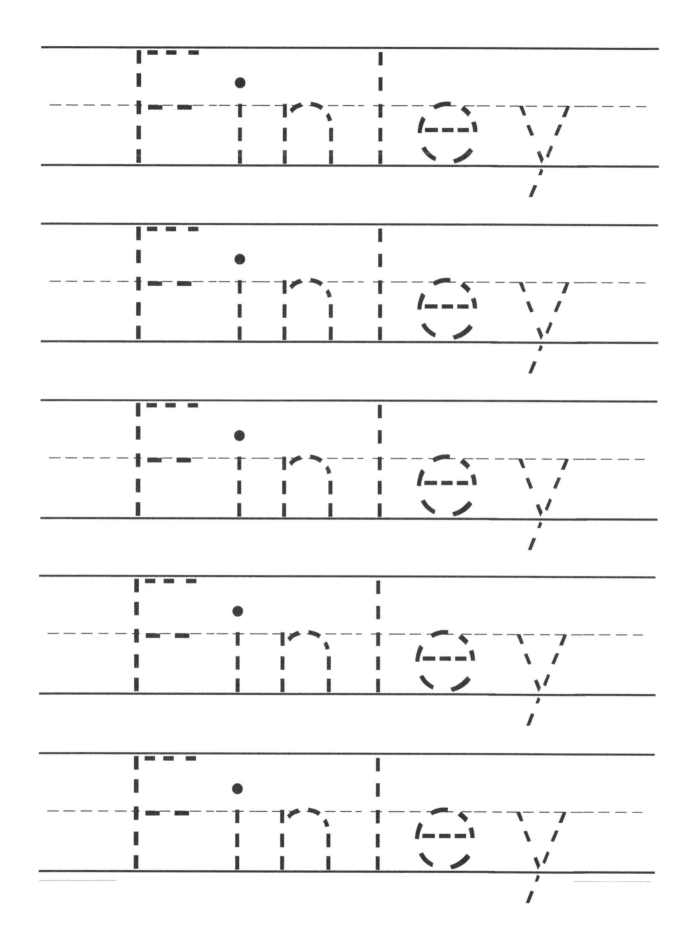

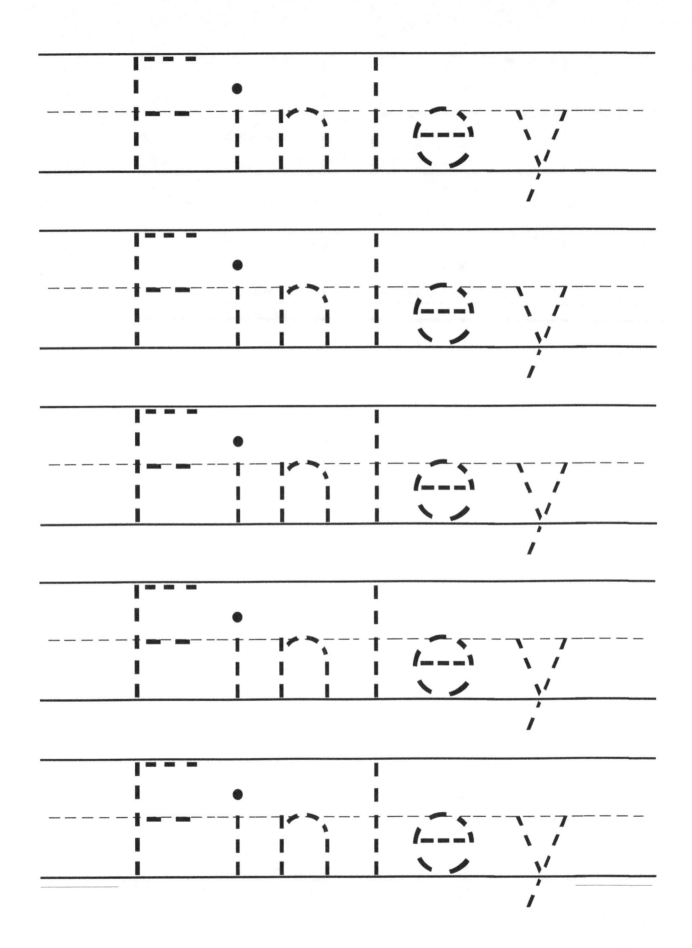

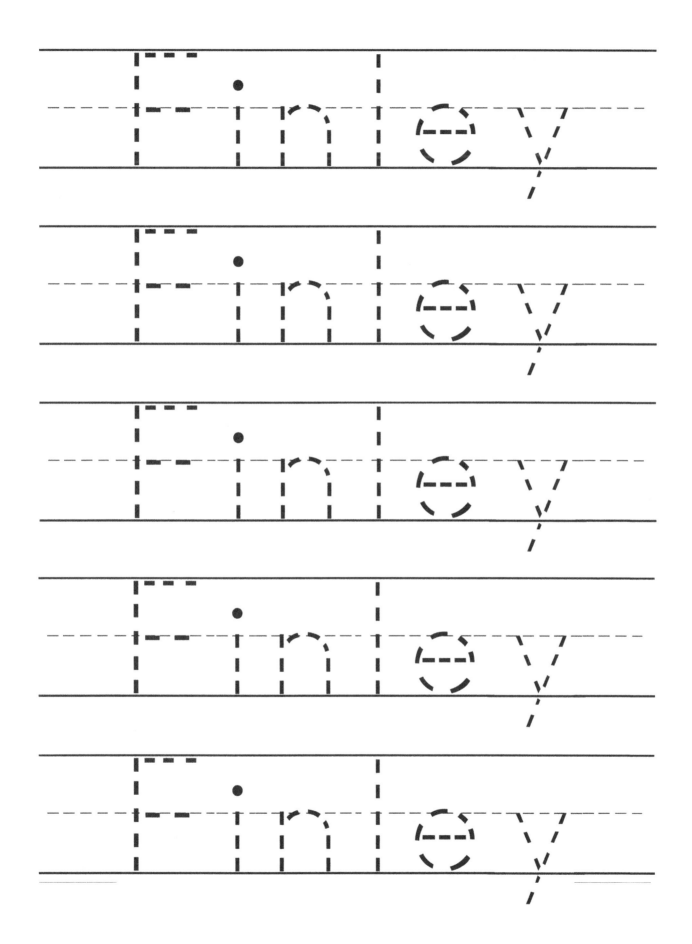

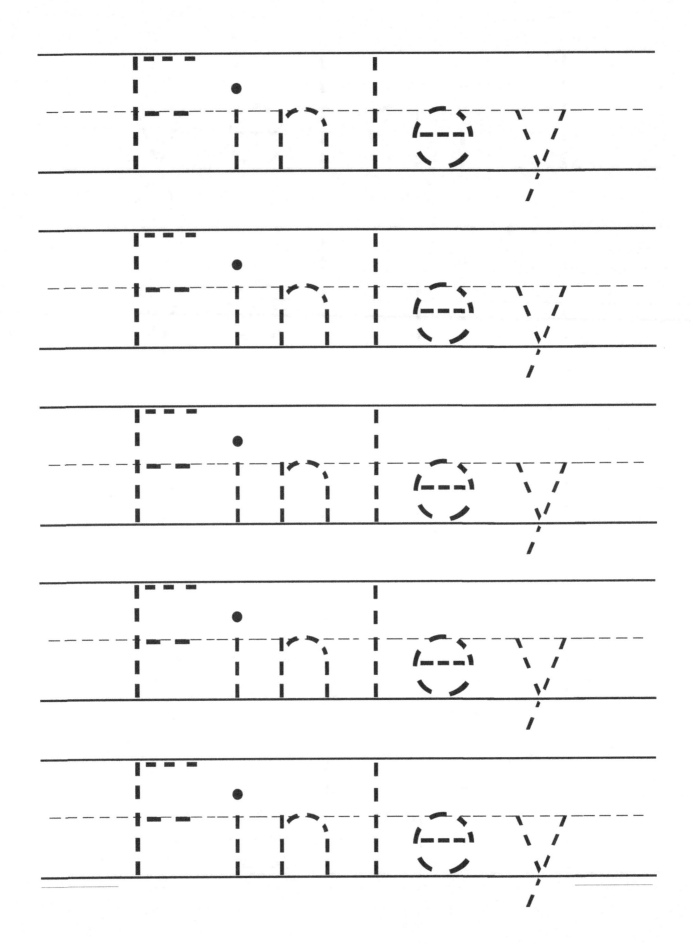

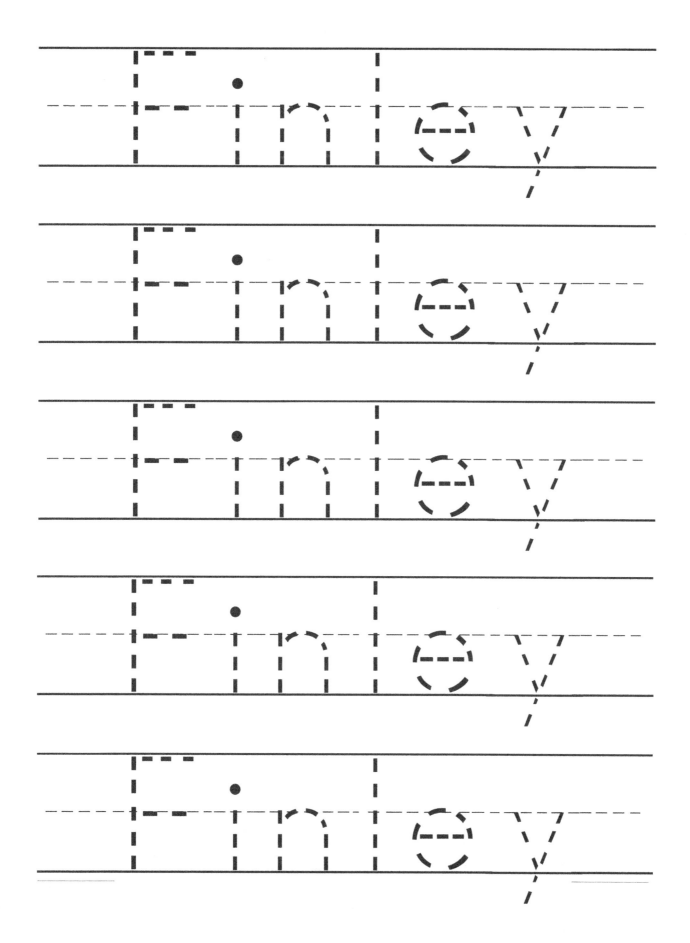

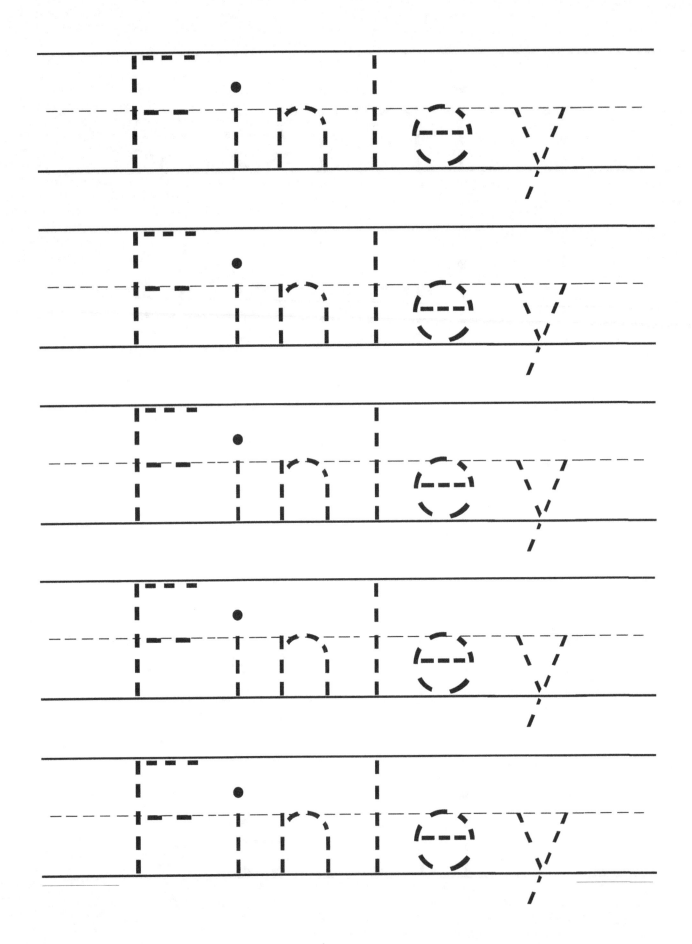

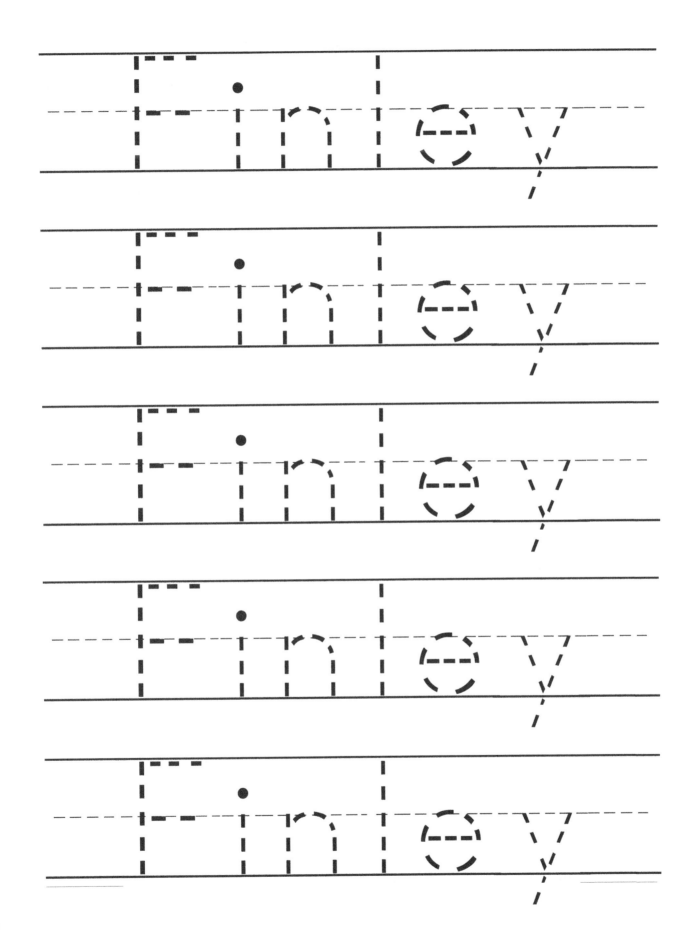

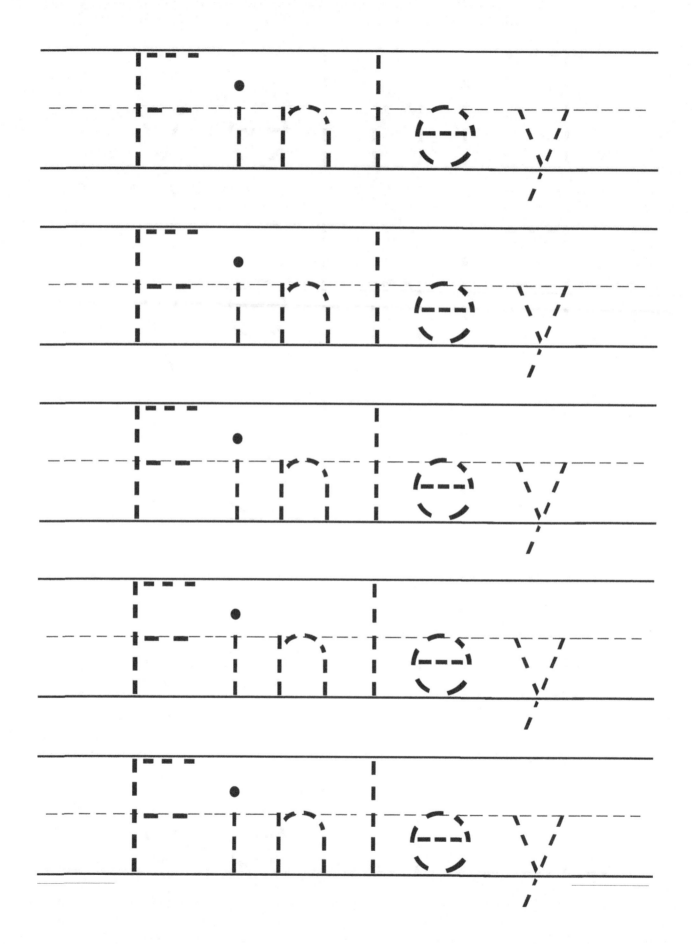

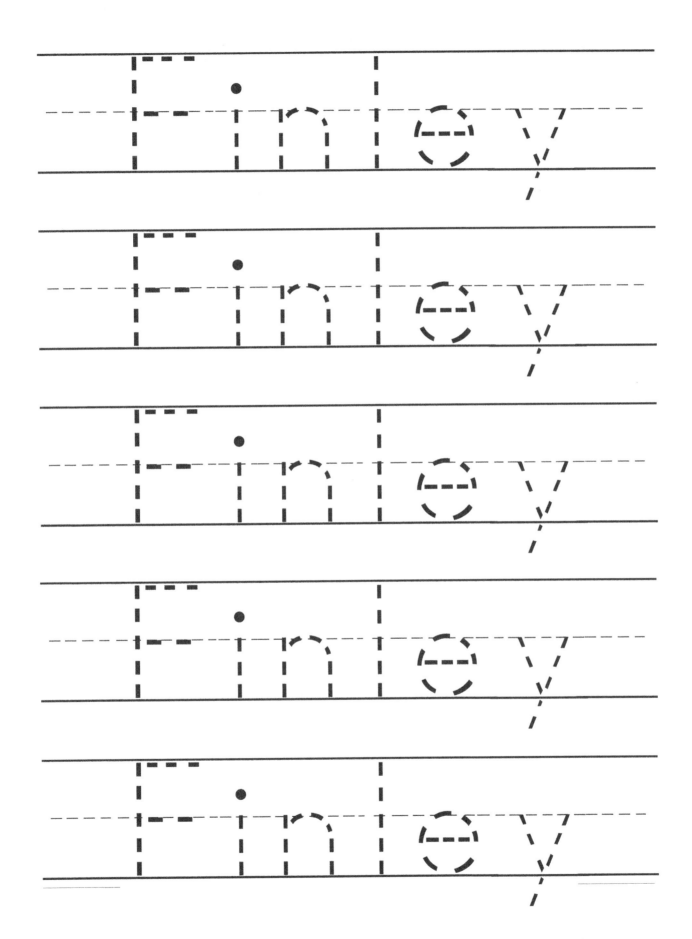

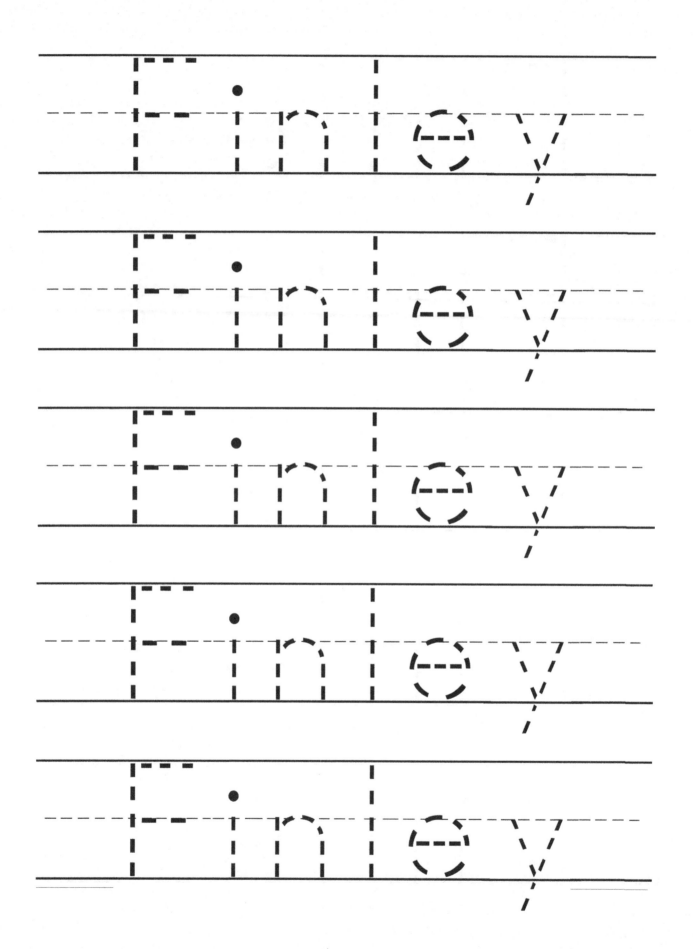

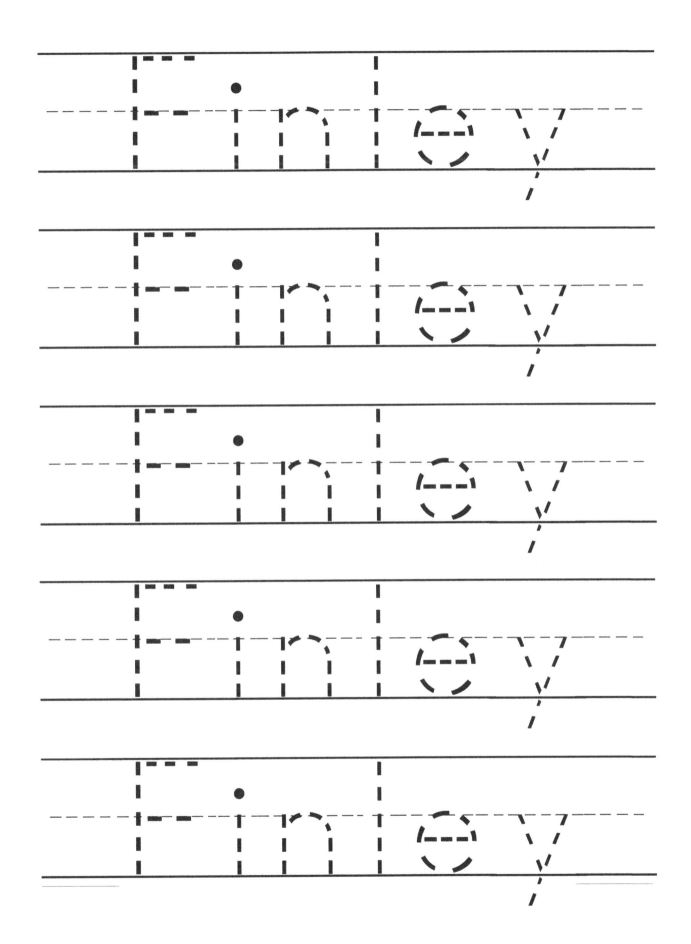

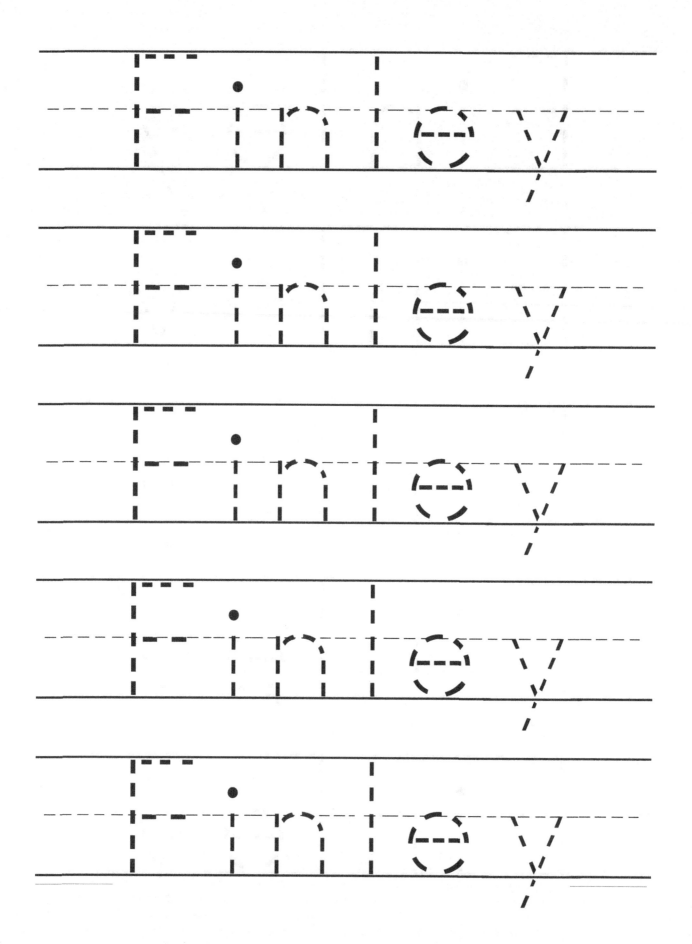

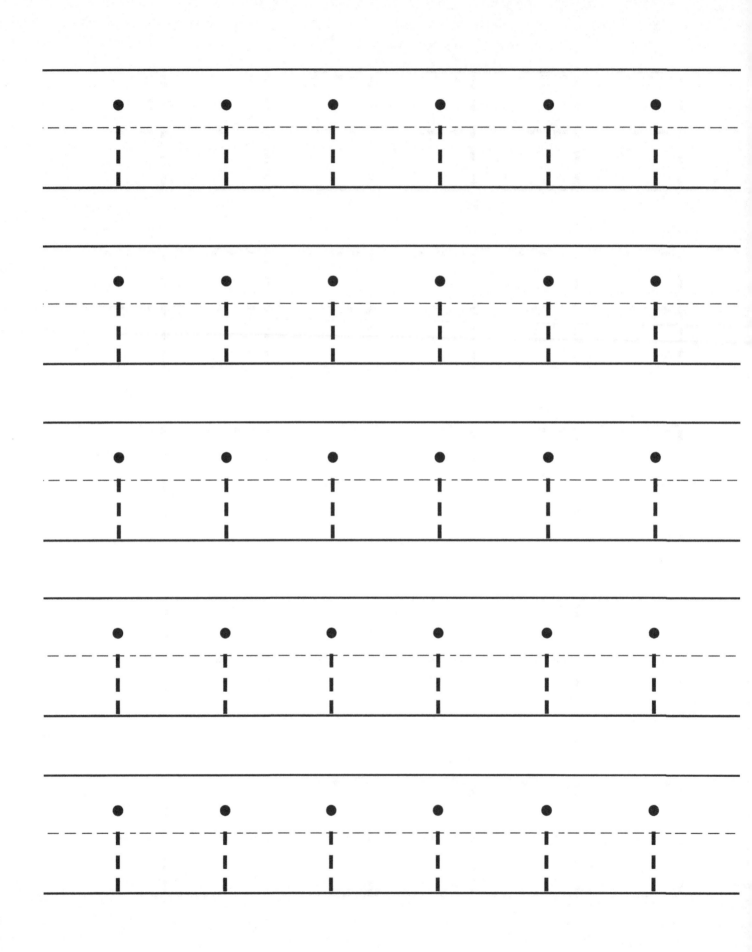

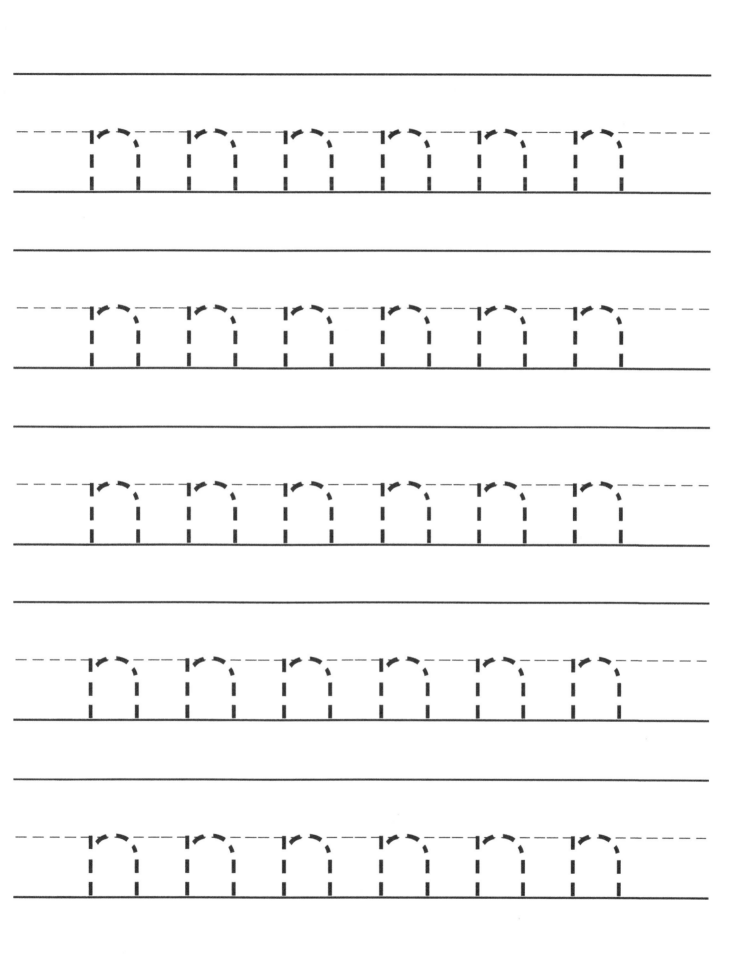

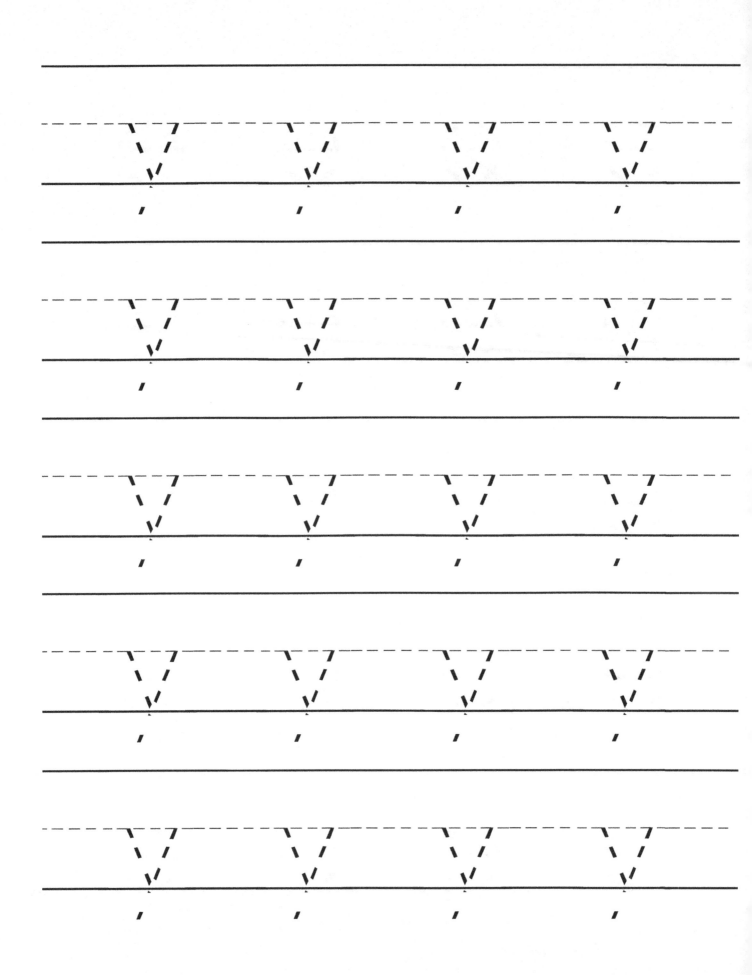

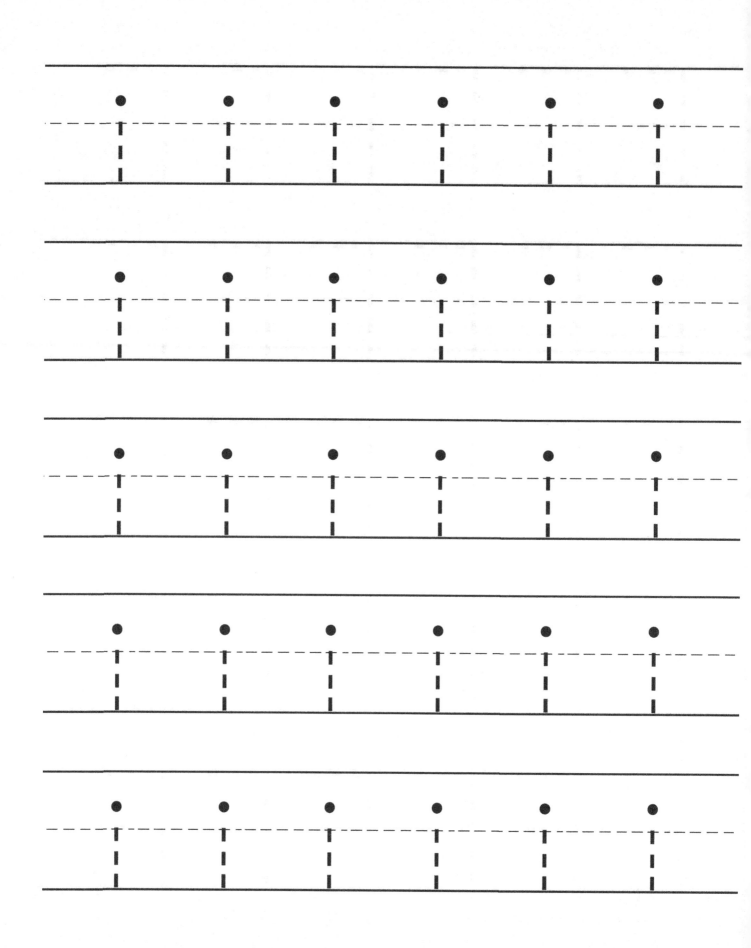

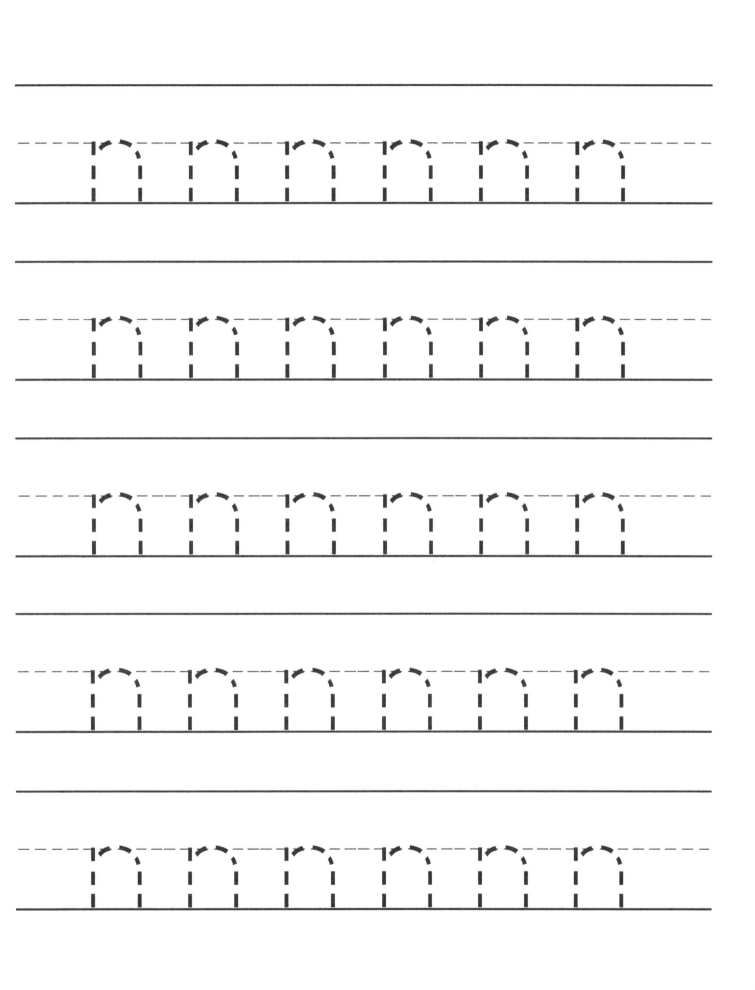

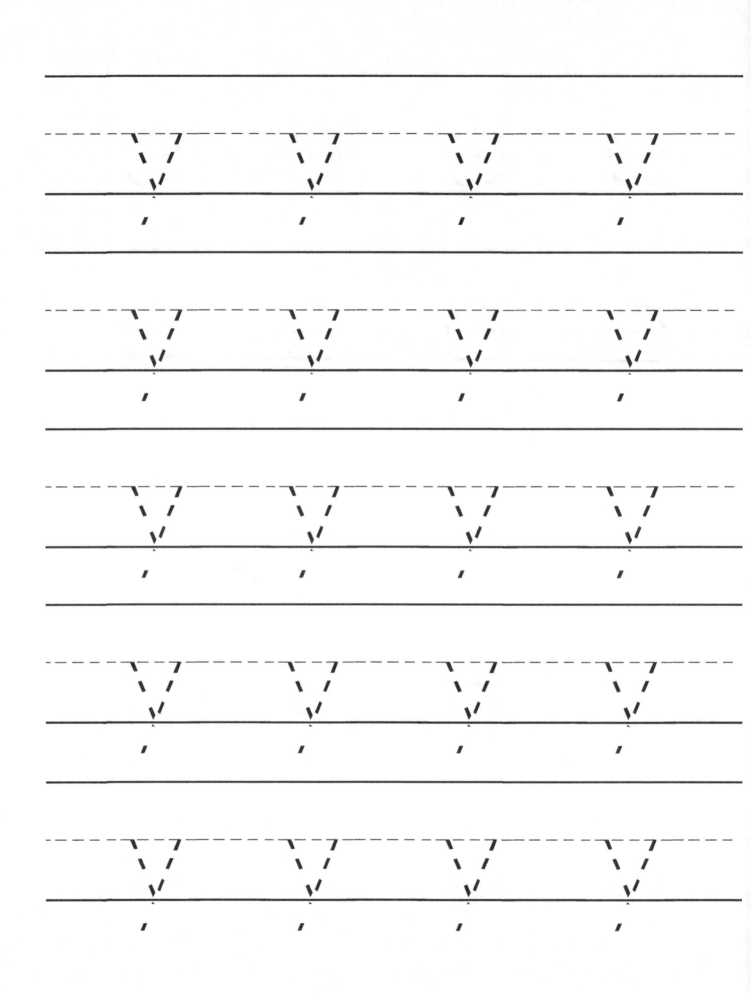

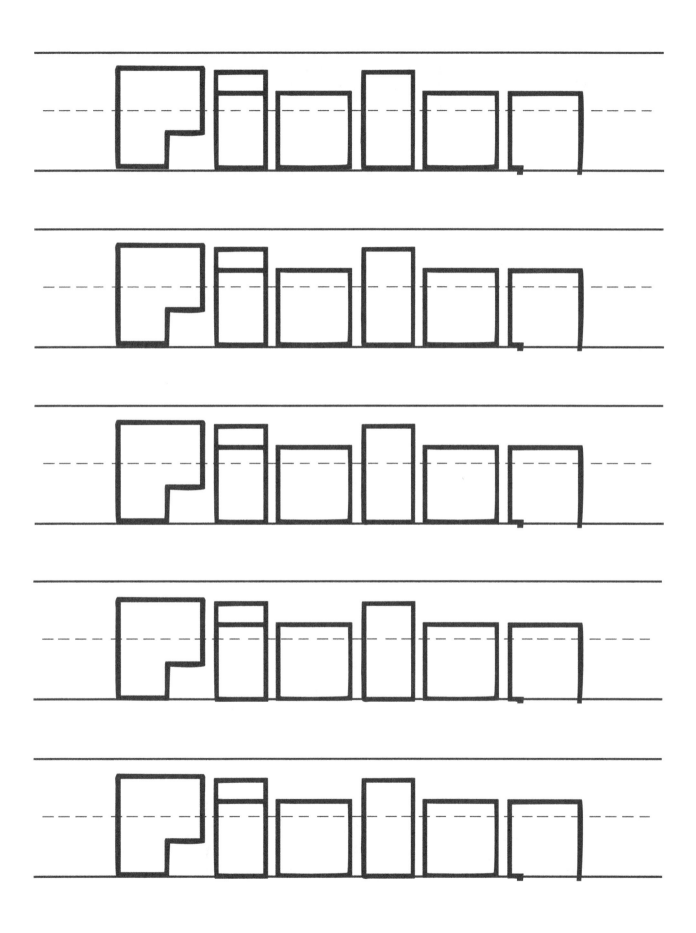

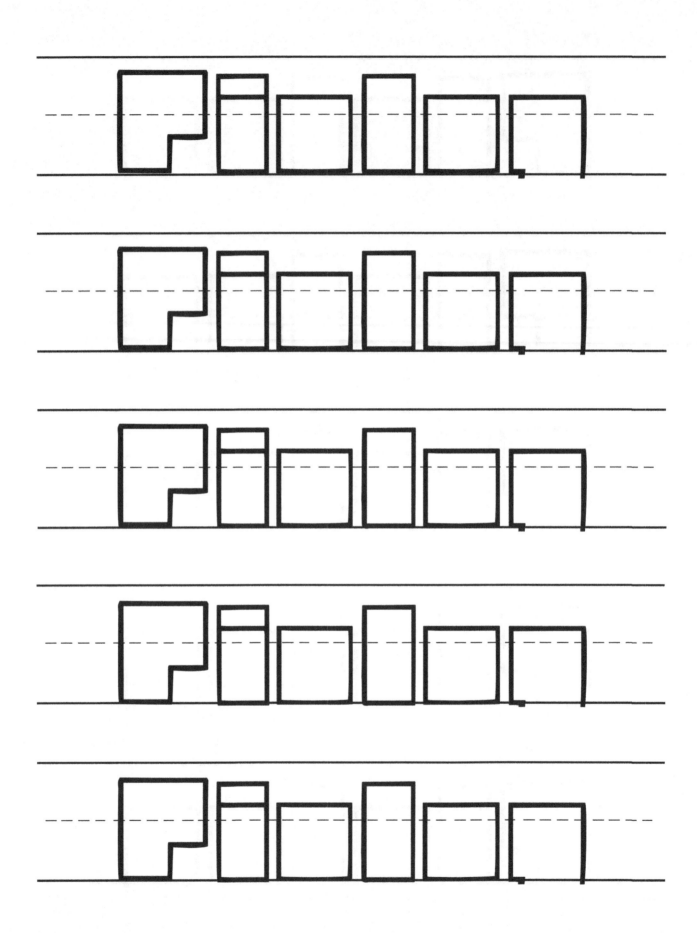

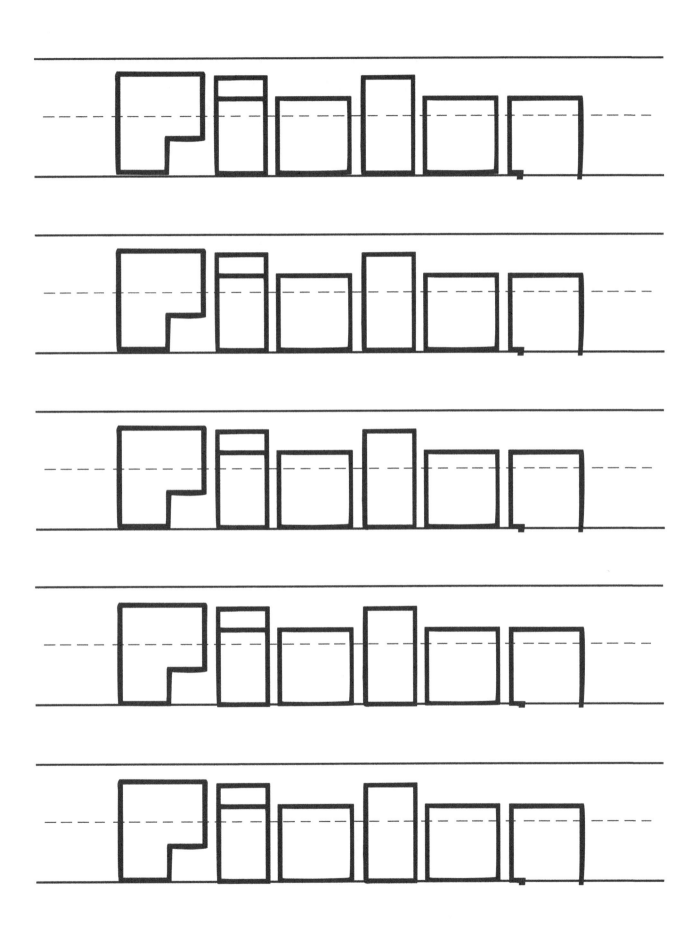

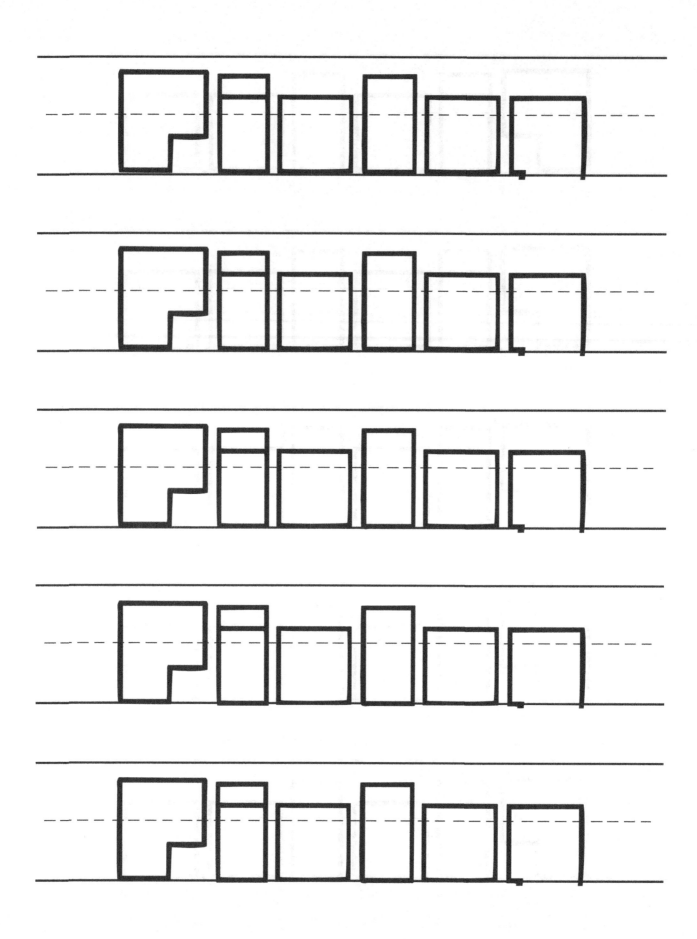

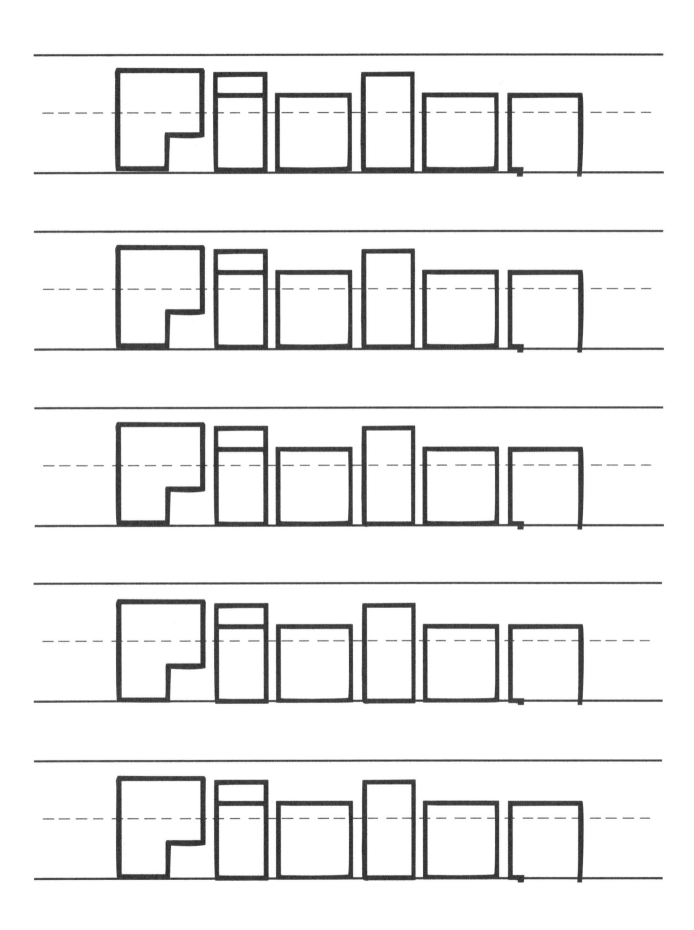

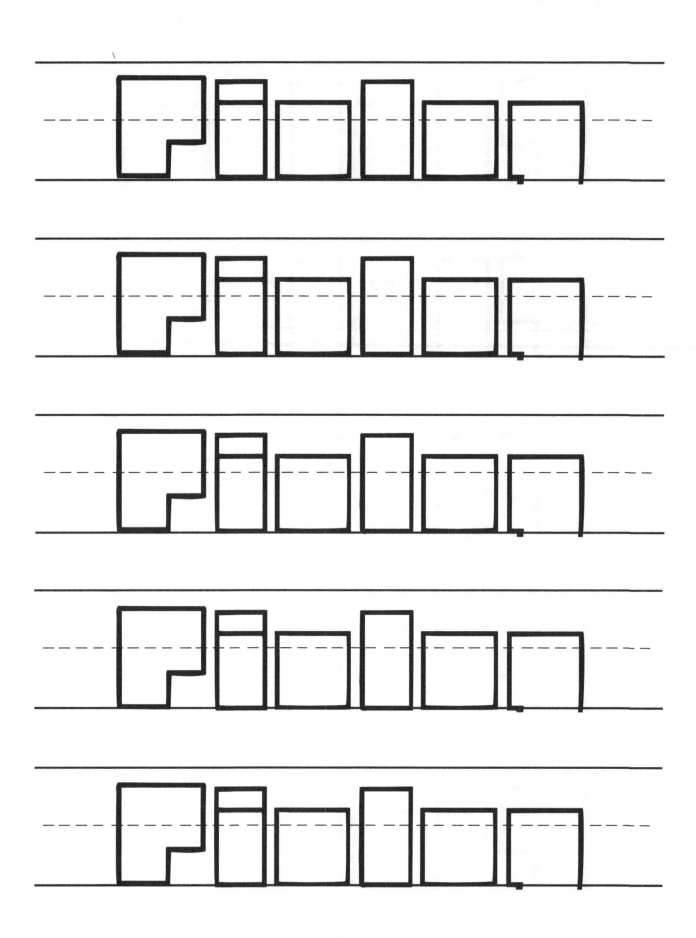

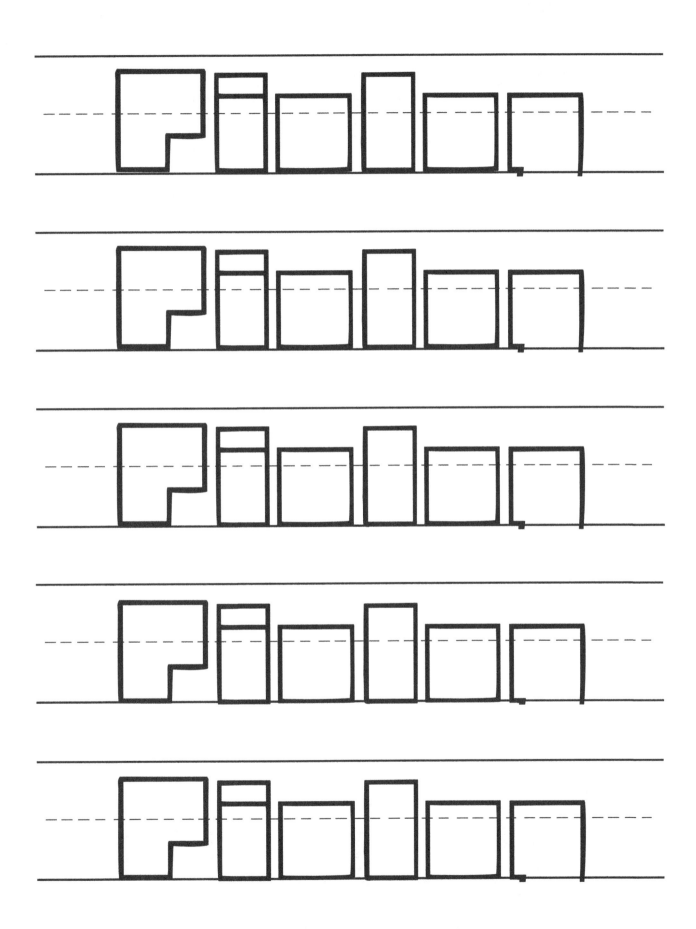

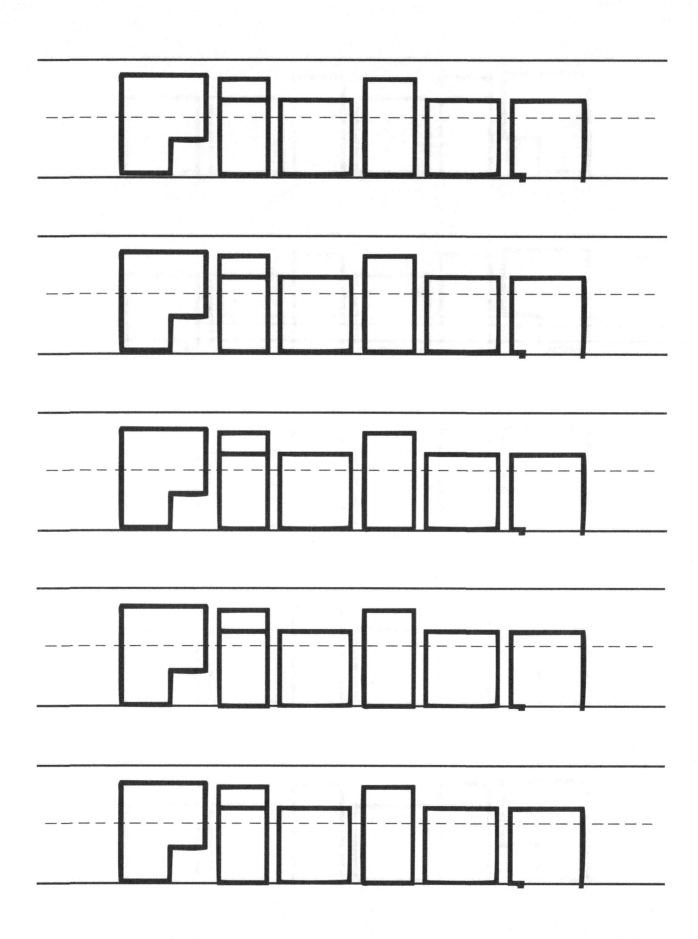

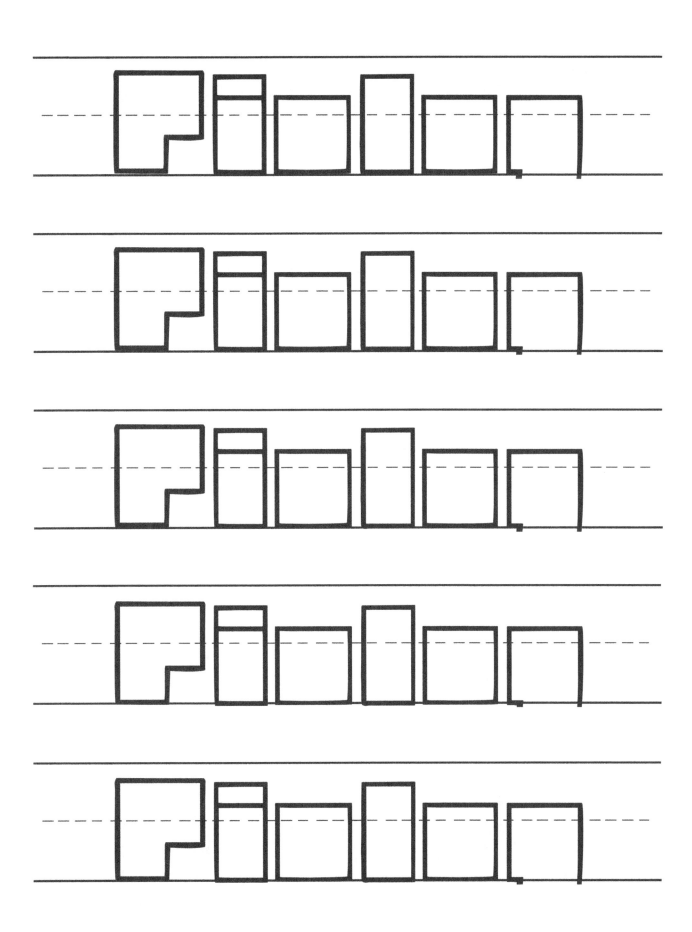

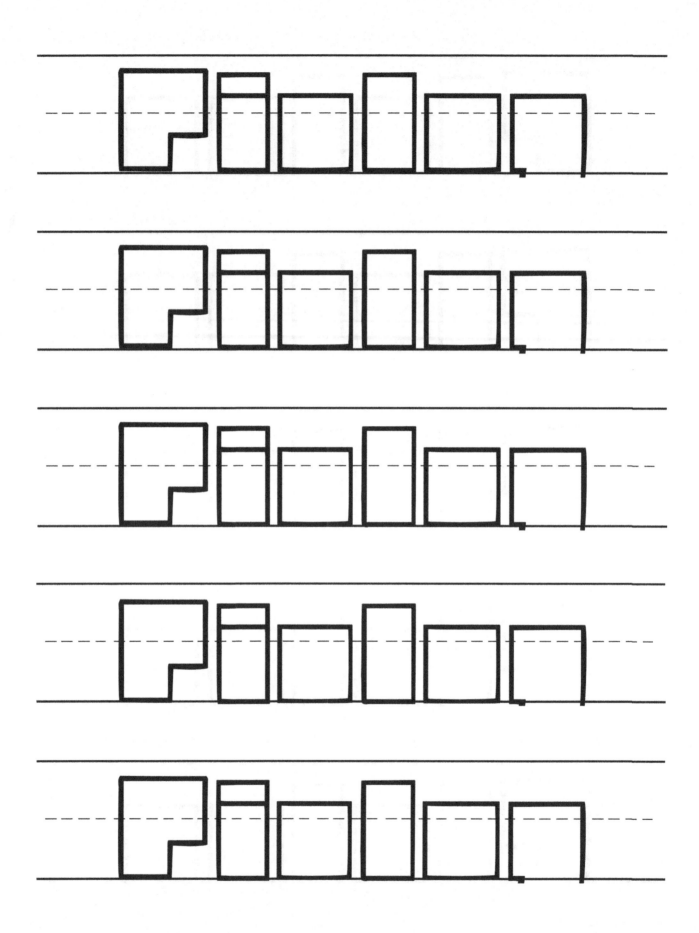

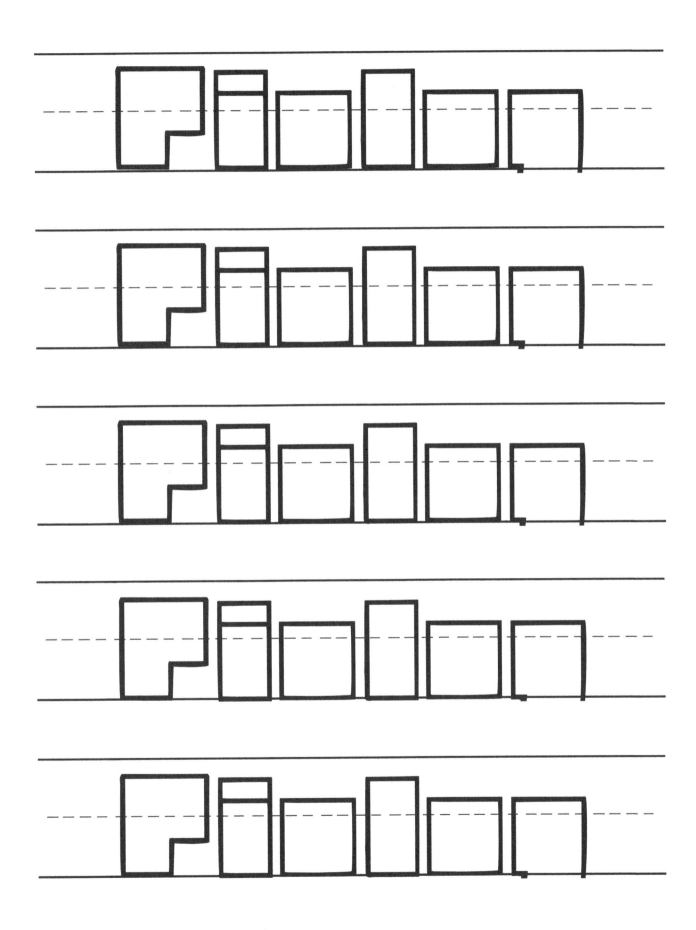

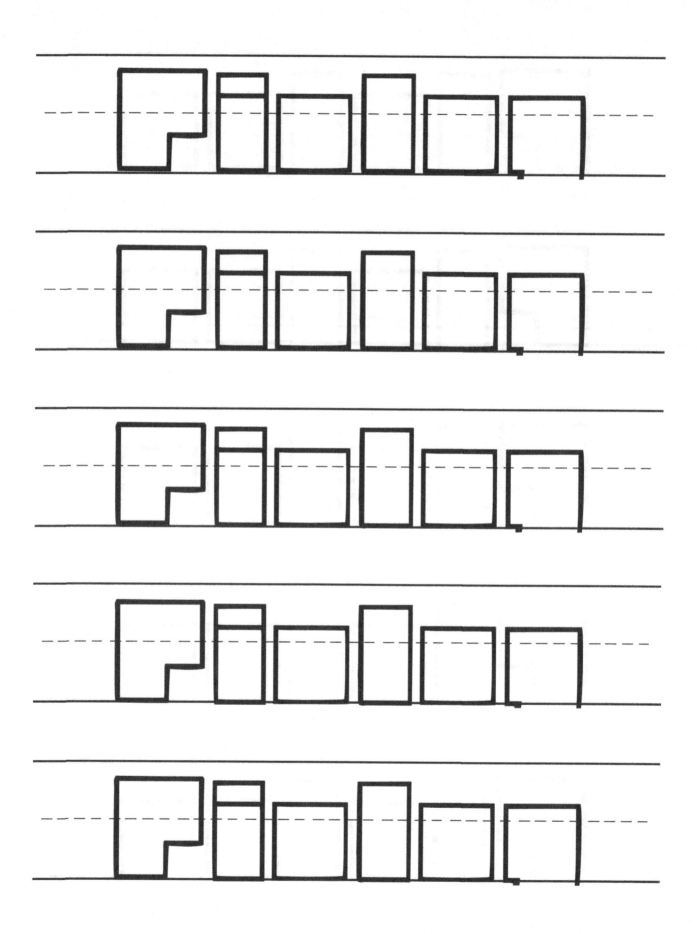

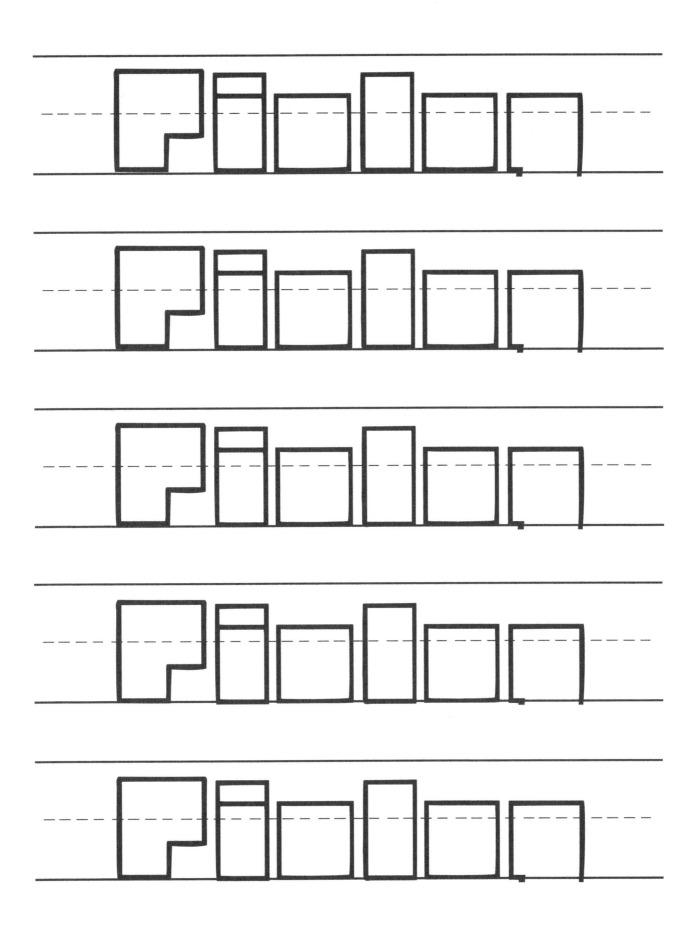

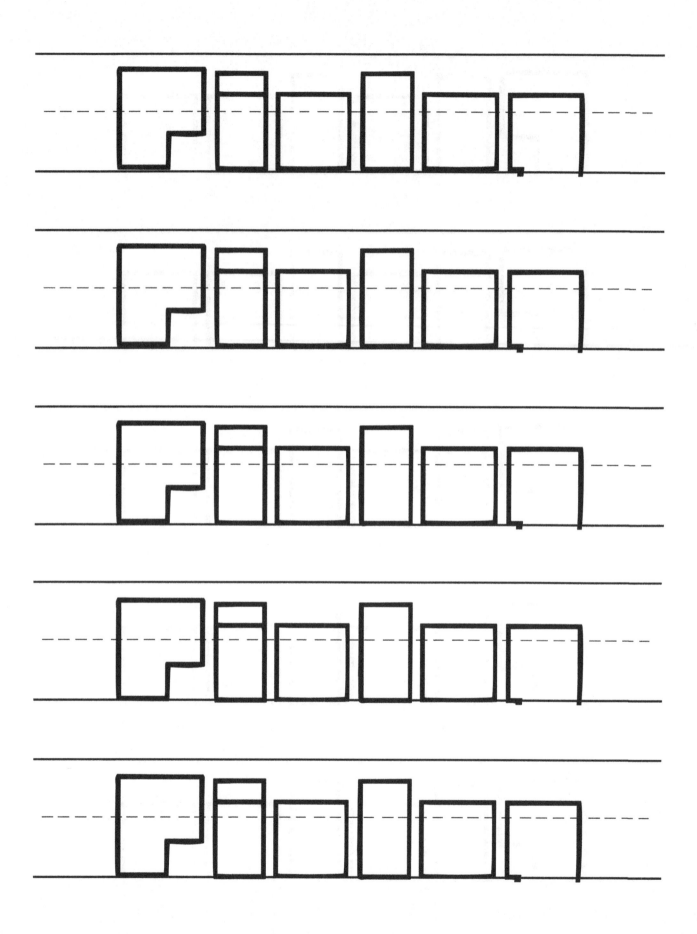

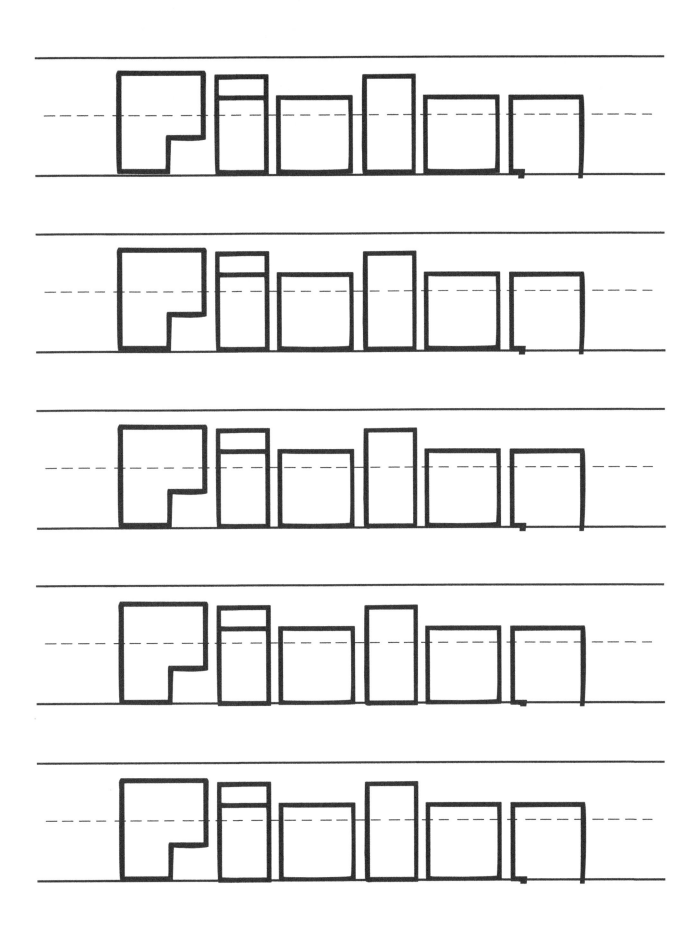

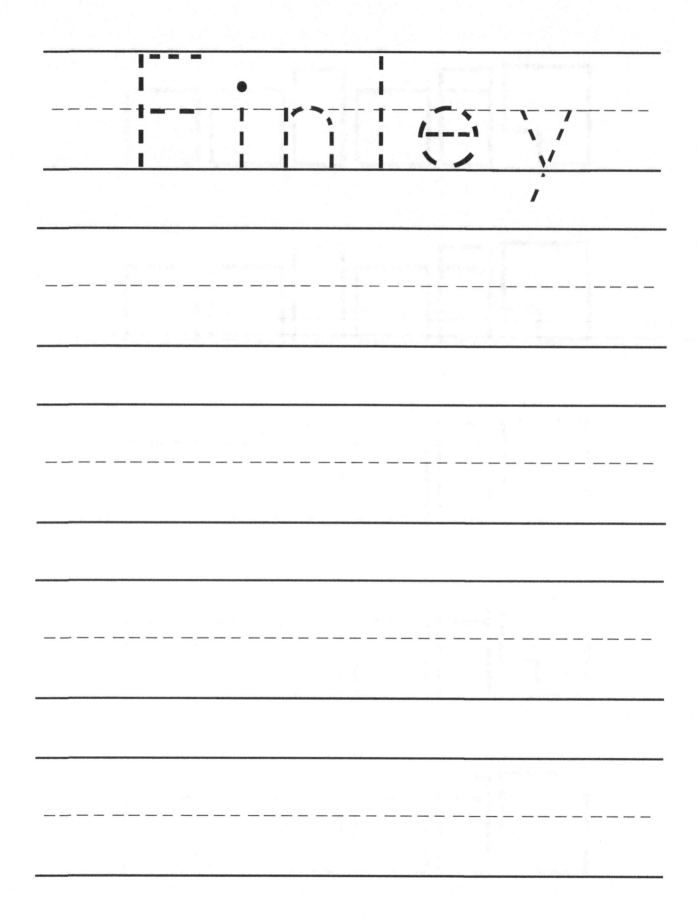

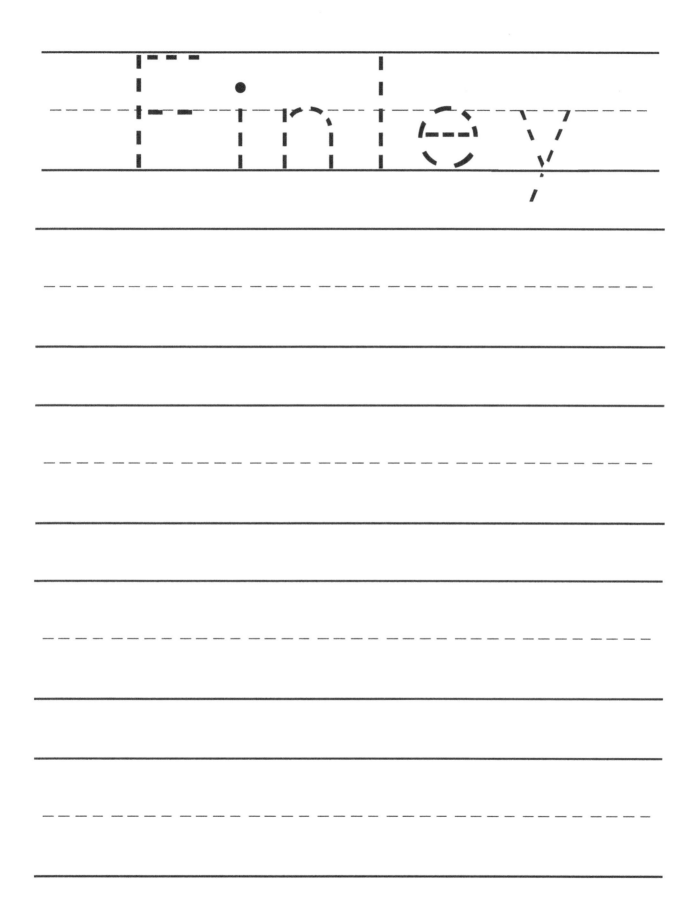

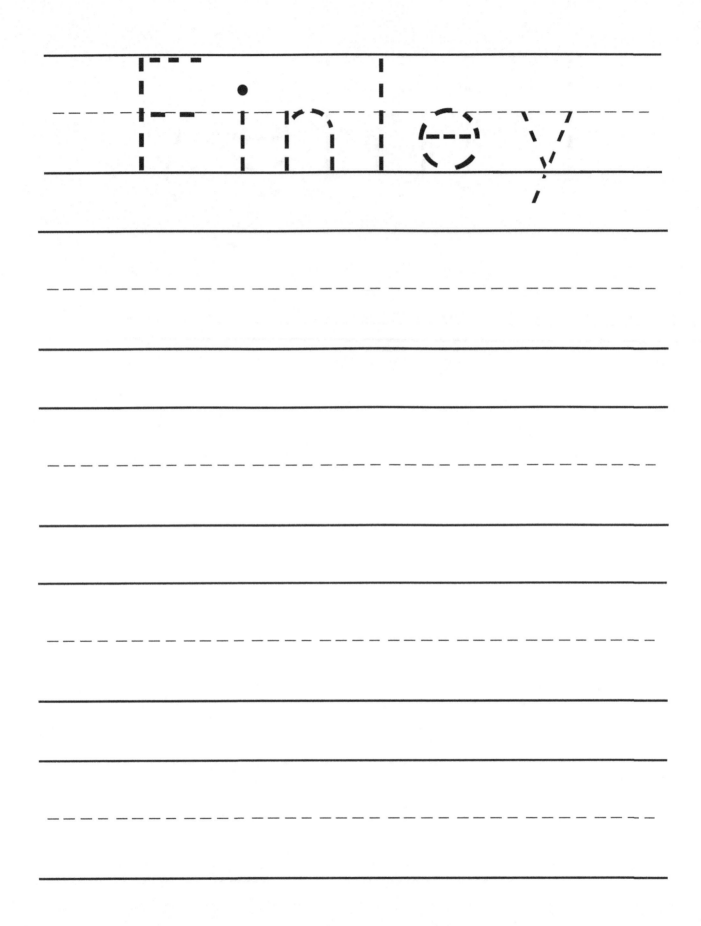

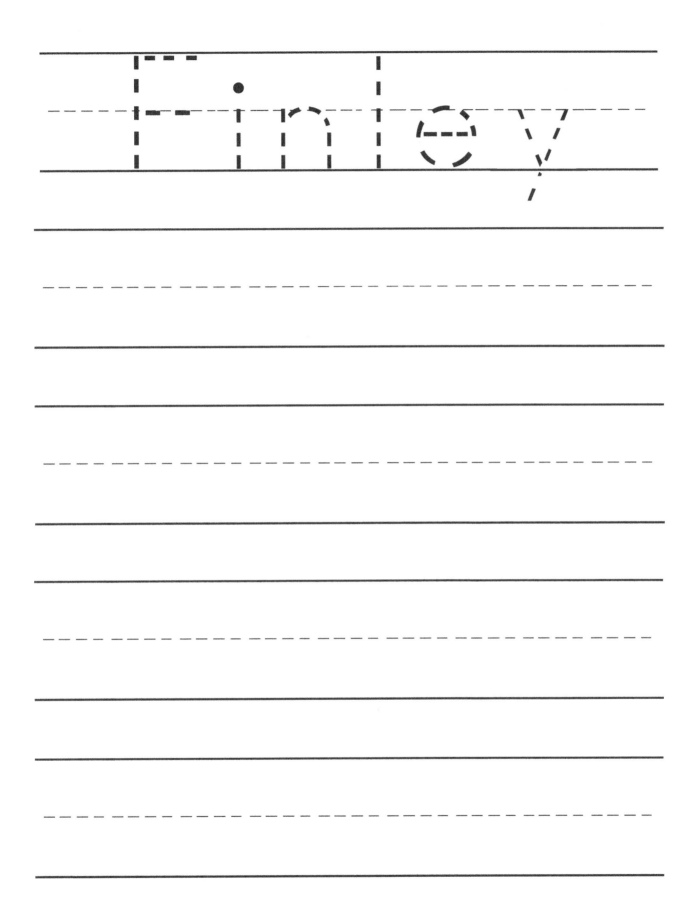

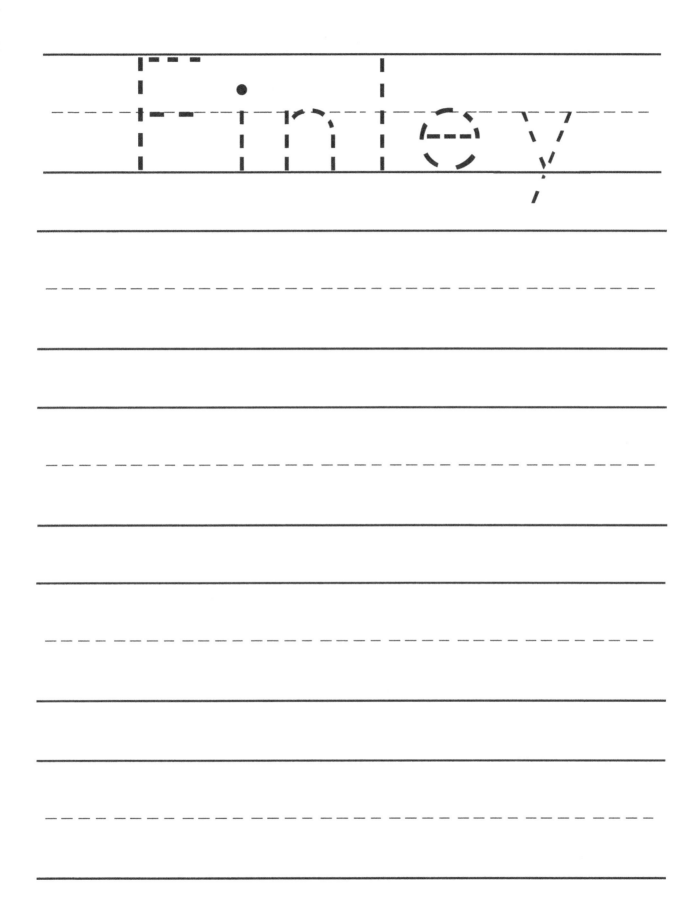

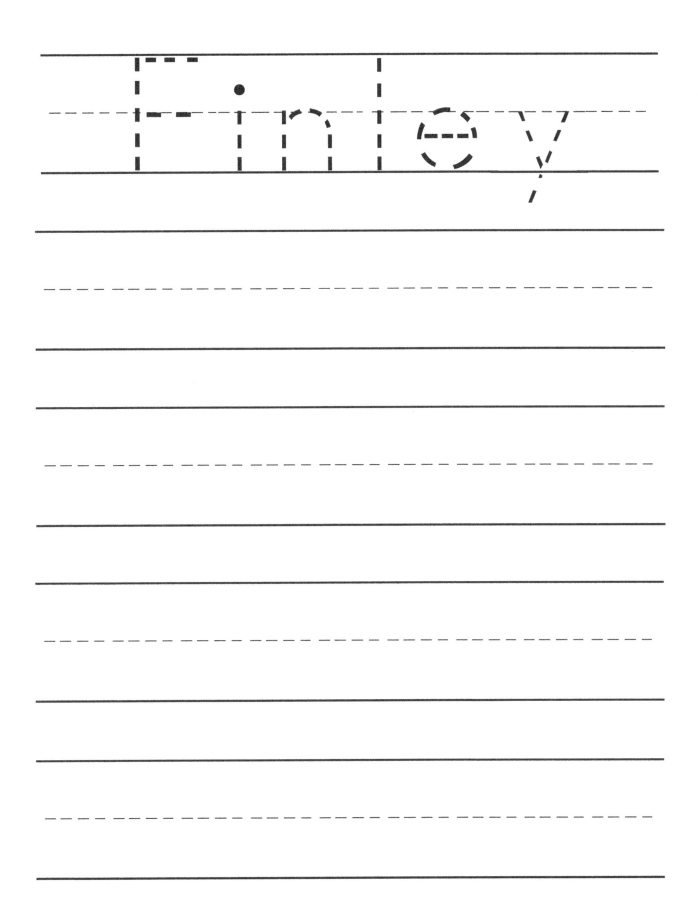

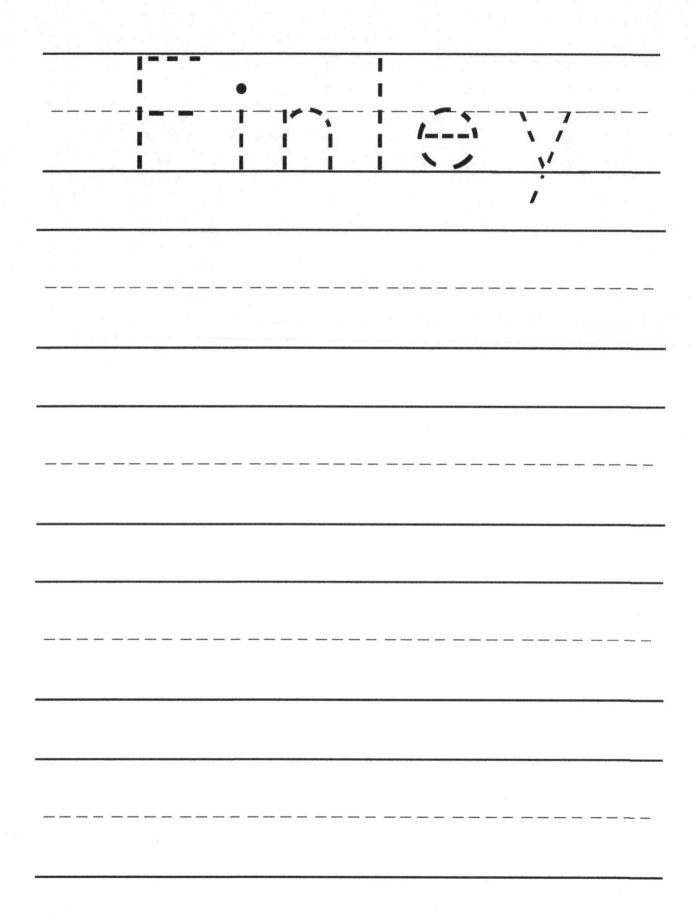

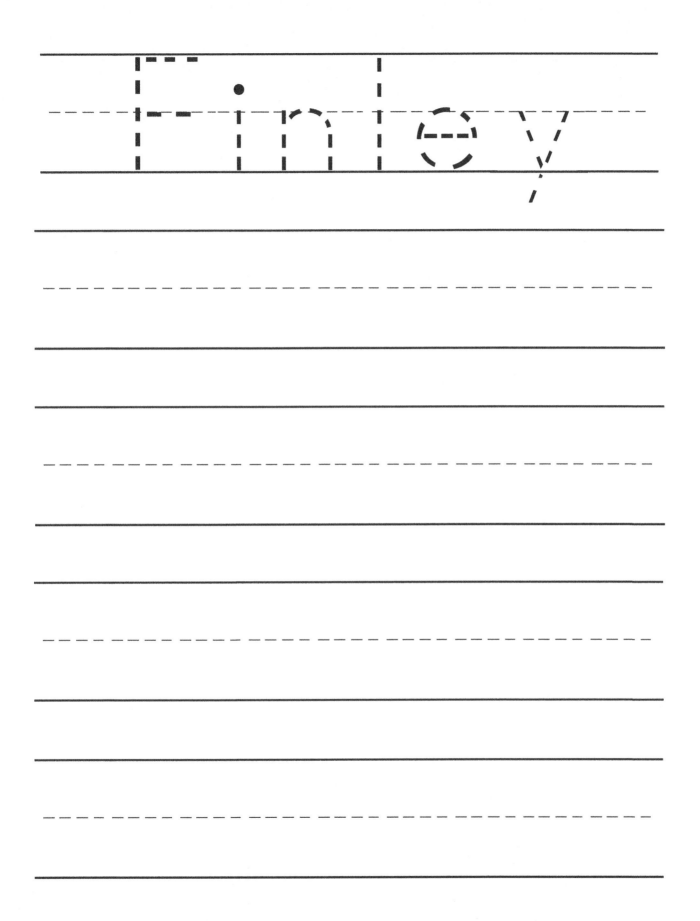

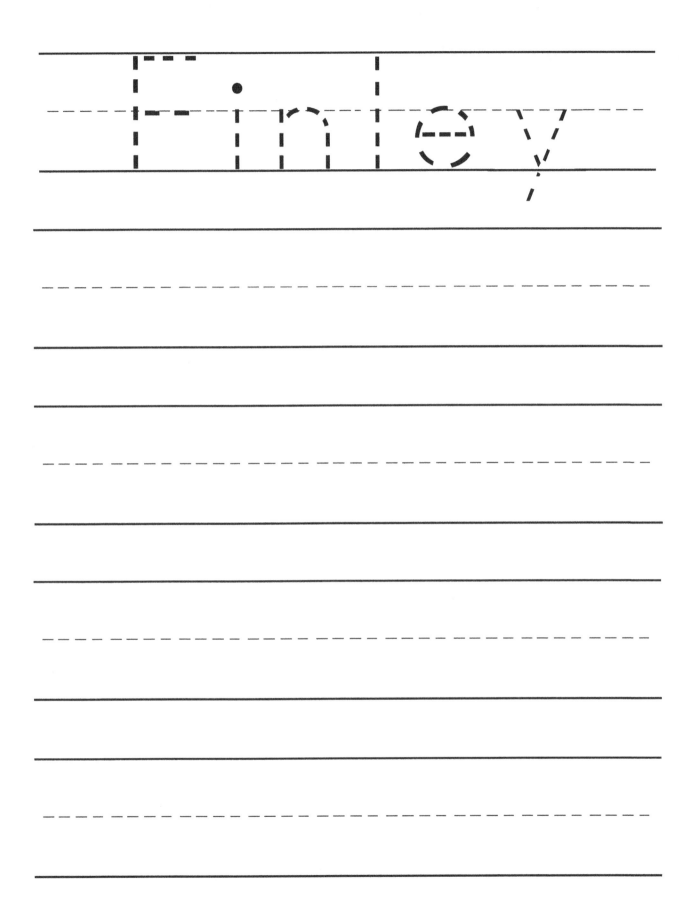

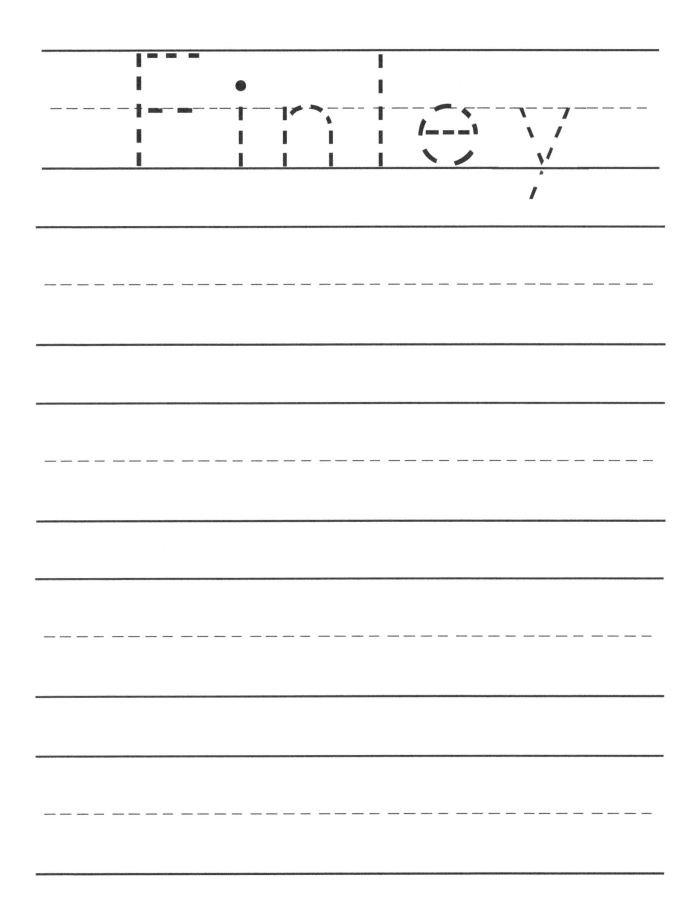

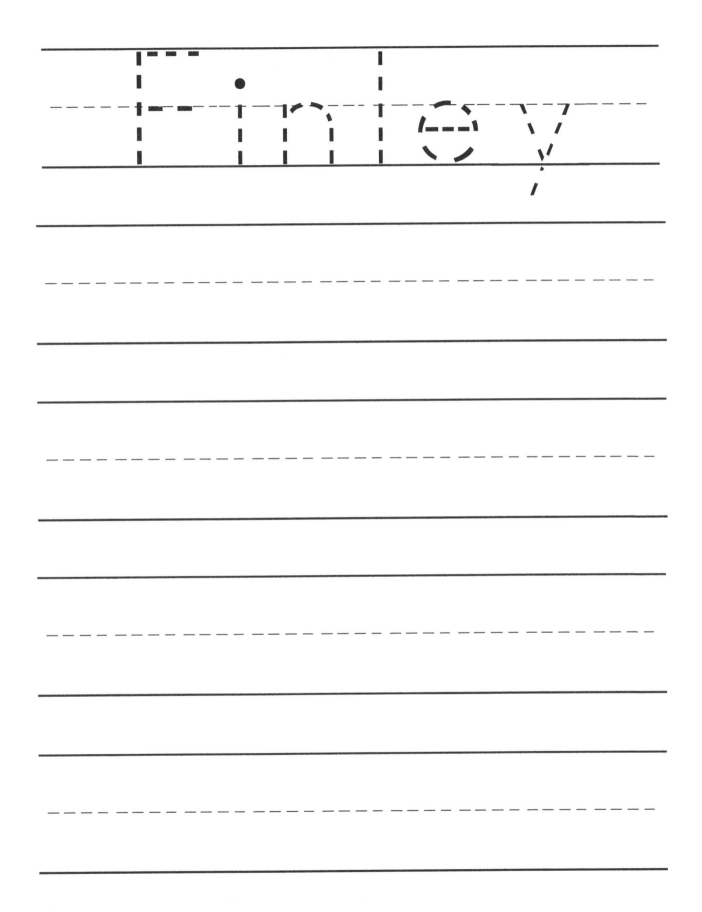

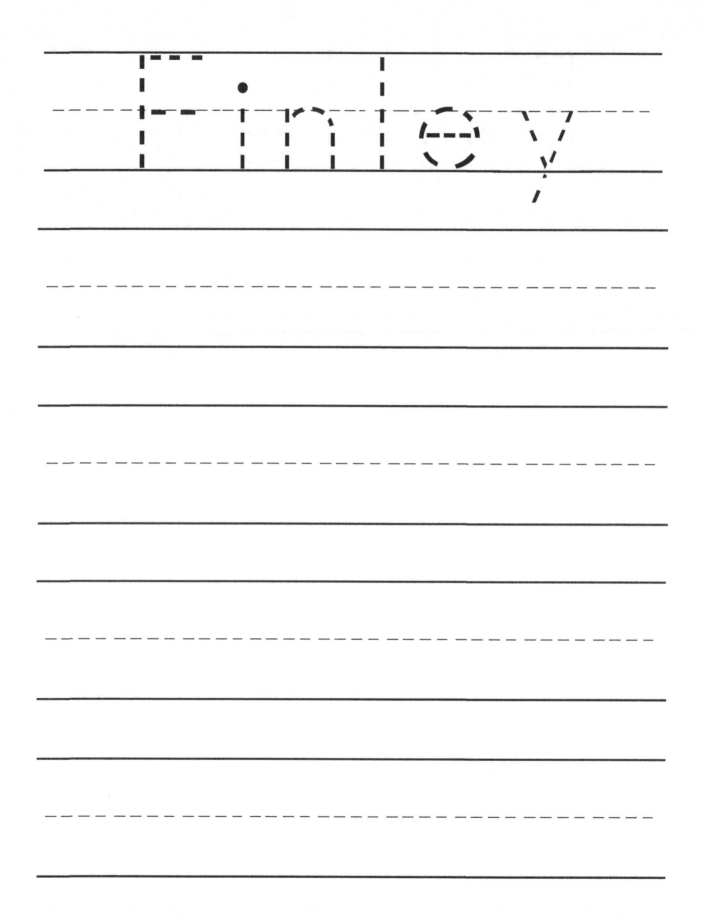

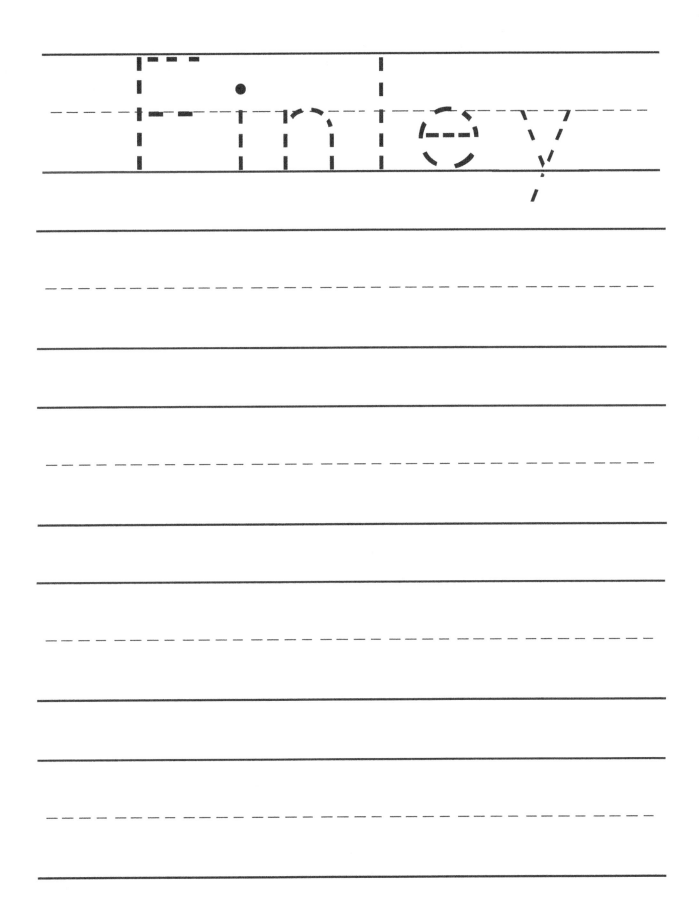

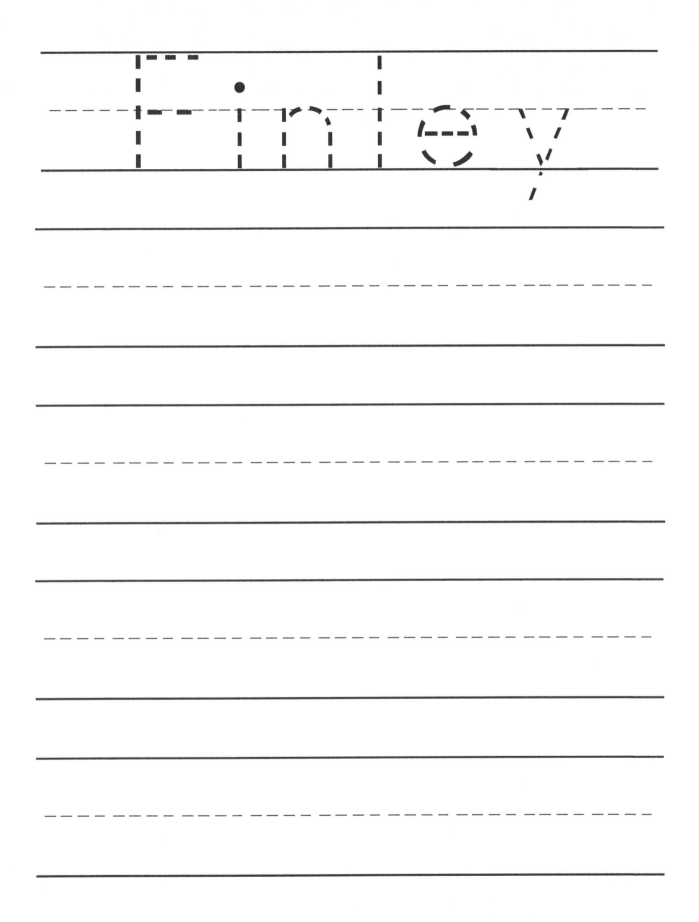

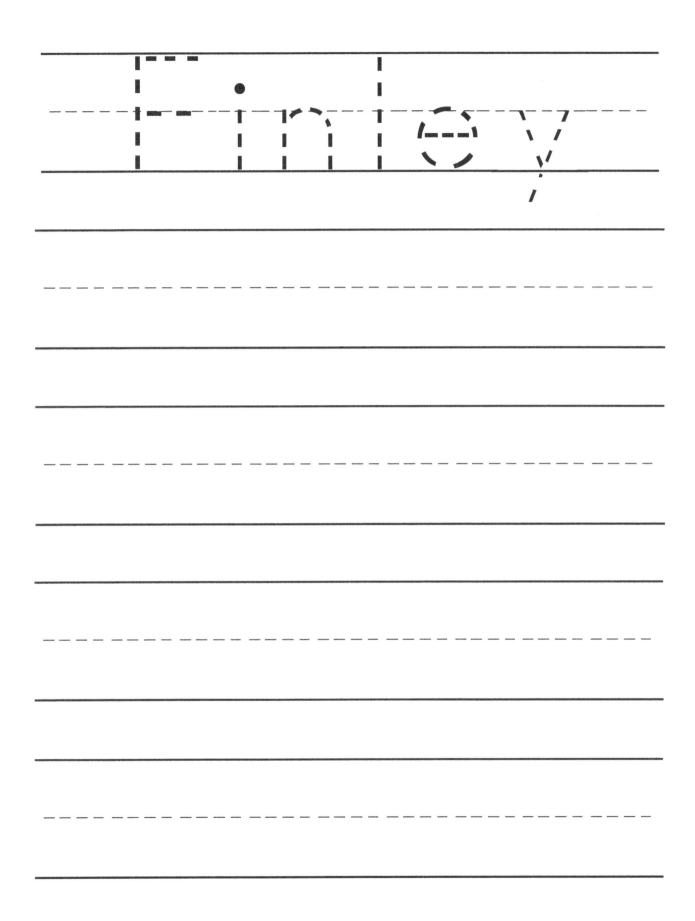

23406105R00057